Brunswick Stew

Best Wishes
Eleanor Hinton

ALSO BY ELEANOR HINTON

Waiting for a Miracle

Brunswick Stew

STORIES AND POEMS FOR THE NEW MILLENNIUM

Edited by and Selections Written
by Eleanor Hinton

With Stories by Contributors to
the NEW YORK TIMES Bestseller
Chicken Soup for the Soul

CHAPEL HILL
PRESS, INC.

ISBN 1-59715-004-5
Library of Congress Catalog Number 2005926808

Printed in the United States of America
First Printing

DEDICATION

This book is dedicated to all the beautiful people who are looking for inspiration in their lives. The stories and poems in *Brunswick Stew* are hearty enough to heal the soul, restore your spirit, and rebuild your hope, giving you the spiritual nourishment and courage you need to help you make it through the day.

I also dedicate this book to my son, Kirk, who has inspired me to be more caring and understanding of others through his struggle with his disability.

CONTENTS

Young Adults

ACKNOWLEDGMENTS

Brunswick Stew was conceived more than two years ago. It has been a rewarding experience creating this book. I am grateful to my deceased grandmother for preparing the hearty, rib-sticking stew for me when I was a child.

A special thanks to the many contributors of stories and poems that are published in *Brunswick Stew*. And a special thanks to the writers who submitted stories but were not published this time.

A sincere appreciation of support and patience to my typist, Ida Batson, who spent many hours typing and retyping the manuscript. Without her the task would have been difficult.

INTRODUCTION

According to research, Brunswick Stew was made as early as 1828 on the bank of the Nottoway River in Virginia. It is said that the stew was made for a group of hunters by the camp's cook, who decided himself to go hunting. Upon returning from his hunt, he made a pot of stew with squirrel, butter, onion, stale bread, and seasoning. The legendary Brunswick Stew is rich, delicious, hearty, and rib-sticking and was considered a hunter's dish, with ingredients varying from one hunter to the next.

James Beard called Brunswick Stew "one of the most famous of American dishes." Lillian Marshall, Kentucky author and food authority, described it as "that imperishable Southern favorite." Marion Harland, a cookbook author, wrote in 1889, "it is named for Brunswick County, Virginia." The city of Brunswick, Georgia challenges the claims from other places and officials maintain the rich stew is their own.

The book *Brunswick Stew* is as hearty, rib-sticking, heartwarming, and healing as the actual stew itself. It contains the kind of stories you need to help you make it through the day—stories to fill your heart and lift your spirits. This book is filled with stories for men, women, and young people alike. The ingredients and flavor of the contributing writers make the book just as varied and interesting as the stew.

Recipe for Brunswick Stew

(From: *Fireside Cooks & Black Kettle Recipes*, Doris E. Farrington, ed., Indianapolis/New York: Bobbi-Merrill, 1976)

Cut up two squirrels (or a three pound chicken) and put in a large pan with three quarts of water, one large sliced onion, one half-pound of lean ham cut in small pieces and simmer gently for two hours. Add three pints of tomatoes, one pint of lima beans, four large Irish potatoes diced, one pint grated corn, one tablespoon salt, one fourth teaspoon pepper, and a small pod of red pepper. Cover and simmer gently for one more hour stirring frequently to prevent scorching. Add three ounces of butter and serve hot.

—Late 18th-century recipe, Richmond, Virginia

BRUNSWICK STEW FOR EIGHT

1 large stewing fowl, cut into pieces
4 cups cold water
1 can condensed tomato soup
1 cup canned tomatoes
1 onion, sliced thin
1 cup green lima beans
3 potatoes, sliced thin
1 teaspoon sugar
Salt and pepper (to taste)
1 cup canned kernel corn
¼ pound butter
Flour (optional)

Simmer fowl for 2 hours. Remove meat from bones and cut into small pieces. Return to kettle and add tomato soup, canned tomatoes, onion, lima beans, potatoes, sugar, and seasoning. Cook until vegetables are tender. Add corn and butter. Cook slowly for about five minutes. Can be thickened with flour-water paste. Add more seasoning to taste.

—Modern adaptation by author

THE GOLDEN CRANE: A SYMBOL OF PEACE

—— Patricia Lorenz ——

Have you ever hear a little voice inside your head or heart telling you to do something you didn't understand? Did you follow that voice?

Art Beaudry, from Milwaukee, Wisconsin, never used to, but something happened to him not long ago that changed all that.

As the teacher of origami (the ancient Japanese art of paper folding) at the LaFargo Lifelong Learning Institute in Milwaukee, Wisconsin, Art was asked to represent the school at an exhibit at a large mall in Milwaukee. He decided to take along a couple hundred folded paper cranes to pass out to people who stopped at his booth.

Before that day, however, something strange happened—a voice told him to find a piece of gold foil paper and make a gold origami crane. The strange voice was so insistent that Art actually found himself rummaging through his collection of origami papers at home until he found one flat, shiny piece of gold foil.

"Why am I doing this?" he asked himself. Art had never worked with foil and certainly didn't understand the strange voice inside him.

When he began to work with the shiny gold paper, it didn't fold as easily or neatly as the crisp multicolored papers. But that little voice kept nudging. He harrumphed and tried to ignore the voice. "Why gold foil anyway? Paper is much easier to work with," he grumbled.

The voice continued. "Do it! And you must give it away tomorrow to a special person."

By now Art was getting a little cranky. "What special person?" he asked the voice.

"You'll know which one," the voice said.

That evening Art very carefully folded and shaped the unforgiving gold foil until it became as graceful and delicate as a real crane about to take flight. He packed the exquisite bird in the box along with the two hundred colorful paper cranes he'd made over the past few weeks.

The next day at the mall, dozens upon dozens of people stopped by Art's booth to ask questions about origami. He demonstrated the art. He folded, unfolded, refolded. He explained the intricate details, the need for sharp creases.

Then there was a woman standing in front of Art. The special person. Art had never seen her before, and she hadn't said a word as she watched him carefully fold a bright pink piece of paper into a crane with pointed, graceful wings.

Art glanced up at her face, and before he knew what he was doing, his hands were down in the big box that contained the supply of paper cranes. There it was, the delicate gold-foil bird he'd labored over the night before. He retrieved it and carefully placed it in the woman's hand.

"I don't know why, but there's a very loud voice inside me telling me I'm suppose to give you this golden crane. The crane is the ancient symbol of peace," Art said simply.

The woman didn't say a word. She slowly cupped her small hand around the fragile bird as if it were alive. When Art looked up at her face, he saw tears filling her eyes, ready to spill out.

Finally, the woman took a deep breath and said, "My husband died three weeks ago. This is the first time I've been out. Today … "she wiped her eyes with her free hand, still gently cradling the golden crane with the other.

She spoke very quietly, "Today is our golden wedding anniversary."

Then this stranger said in a clear voice, "Thank you for this beautiful gift. Now I know that my husband is at peace. Don't you see? That voice you heard, it's the voice of God and this beautiful crane is a gift from Him. It's the most wonderful 50th wedding anniversary present I could have received. Thank you for listening to your heart."

And so that's how Art learned to listen very carefully when a little voice within him tells him to do something that he may not understand at the time.

He's sure that the masters of origami from centuries ago also learned the lesson of listening to the little voice in their hearts as they folded the wings of thousands upon thousands of paper cranes—symbols of peace to all generations.

CLARA

—— *Eleanor Hinton* ——

A couple of weeks before the Fourth of July, my pondering over how to spend the holiday was shortened when I received a call from my cousin in Bethesda. She invited me to a cookout at her house on July the fifth. This year, the fourth fell on a Saturday, the perfect weekend holiday. So I wondered why in the world she'd schedule her picnic for that Sunday when everyone would be packing up to beat the traffic and get home.

I decided to be a sport and didn't question her plans. Instead, I planned my long weekend around the Sunday cookout. I figured I'd drive up to Baltimore on Friday to see the Inner Harbor, see the fireworks at the Washington Monument on the fourth and find time to visit a few friends. I had lived in Maryland for thirty years and this would be the perfect opportunity to see a few of the people that I missed so much.

Several days before my trip, when I called my cousin to confirm, I found out that her July fifth picnic had a dual purpose: we were celebrating our nation's birthday, but we were also celebrating the birthday of Clara, a special friend of my cousin. My cousin told me a bit about the woman and I remember thinking, at the time, that she must be exceptional.

The holiday weekend finally came and after all of my other festivities, I arrived at my cousin's house. As I started through the side gate, I was immediately greeted by a raspy voice: "Hello, I'm Clara."

I introduced myself, but more than anything I had food on my mind, so I went in search of picnic fare. Some time later, full and rested, I decided to mingle. My cousins introduced me to some friends from New York and I found myself working my way toward the place where Clara sat with her sister-in-law.

At first I made small talk about their car trip from New York to Maryland and then I met four of Clara's sons. Before I knew it, I had been talking to Clara and her sister-in-law for two hours. This really was an exceptional woman. Not only had she raised seven of her own sons, but she had also adopted two children and fostered two children with fetal alcohol syndrome. She had also used her time to mother many children in her community.

Now, at the age of seventy, she filled her time caring for a ninety-one-year-old woman. It occurred to me, after spending time with Clara, that it was her faith in God and her sense of humor that enabled her to be the kind of person that she was. I really wanted some of her humanitarianism to rub off on me. And finally I realized what I hadn't noticed in any of my holiday planning: this July fifth picnic was really what America is all about—America isn't about having a picnic on a certain day or fireworks or food, those are just symbols of the celebration. America is about people like Clara, it is about the way that Clara has given all of her life and continues to give, joyfully and happily. That's what America means to me and I will keep that in my heart.

MIRACLE MOMENTS

—— Donna Wick ——

Where there is love, there is life. —GANDHI

I remember the day I got the call from my church giving me my first assignment. I had put my name on the list for hospital volunteers and, even though I had no prior experience of volunteering in this way, I was excited to visit Emily that coming Sunday at the Medical Center in Houston.

I decided to visit her right after church and even bought some books at the bookstore so we could spend the day talking about books, the spiritual path, and other things she might enjoy. I knew nothing about her. I didn't even know how old she was, but I knew that we would fast be friends.

I encountered no traffic on the way there and found a parking space right up front and thought, "Wow! God must really be with me today!"

Finding the room was no problem and I gently pushed open the door, but I was not prepared for what I would find inside the room.

The room was dark except for the stream of light coming from

7

the still open doorway. The room had an overwhelming stench almost too much to bear. The light from the doorway pierced through the darkness enough to illuminate the sweet face of Emily, a woman in her 90's, only to show a thin and frail woman whose face was whiter than the crisp white hospital sheets that swallowed her.

"Emily?" I asked, almost hoping I was in the wrong room. Pushing the door open even wider, I was able to notice all the tubes running to and from her little body. She did not answer. She did not move. She hardly breathed. Seeing all this, with my hands still clutching the little bag from my church bookstore, I quickly left the room and propped myself up against the wall there in the hallway.

Gasping for a fresh breath of air, I prayed silently with tears streaming down my cheek. "Dear God, why this? I don't know anything about this. This is my first time to even volunteer. Why give me something so stark, so dismal? I want to do you work, God. I want to do your will, but this, God, I simply cannot do!"

Then God answered in the sweetly compassionate and gentle voice one might expect, saying, "Donna, do you think I would ask you to heal the well? Do you think I would ask for you to feed those already full? Do you think I would ask you to love the loved? Do you think I would ask you to do something that I did not know, beyond all doubt, you were capable of doing?"

How I found the courage, I do not know, but I went back into Emily's room. I clicked on the overhead bed light so that a dim glow illuminated the room. Emily blinked. Then blinked again. Then she opened her eyes.

"Hi Emily, my name is Donna. I've come to visit you," I whispered.

Emily's eyes grew wide, then crinkled at the corner as she smiled. What beautiful eyes Emily had. They were a soft green color outlined in blue. Emily was beautiful.

I put the bag of books on the floor. The tubes coming from Emily's mouth clearly indicated Emily would not be able to carry on any conversation. I thought to myself, "OK God, I came back … now what do I do?"

The thought came to me to pull open her bedside drawer. I did so and took out a small tube of lotion. I poured the lotion in my hand and then rubbed my hands together to warm the lotion. I began to rub lotion on Emily's dry arms. As I did I sang a little phrase to her over and over, "Oh, I know a woman named Emily. She is so dear and sweet to me." As I sang, I felt that this must be the Divine feeling of love held by God for sweet Emily. That indeed Emily was precious to Him, as all of us are.

I pulled back the sheet to rub lotion on her spindly legs. Still singing and glancing back, I checked Emily's face for any sign of discomfort. What I noticed was a small tear coming from her beautiful eyes.

"This feels so good to rub you, Emily. Thank you for letting me rub lotion on you," I whispered.

Her face glowed.

After the lotion was thoroughly rubbed in, I searched the drawer for a brush and began to brush Emily's hair. I dared not raise her up, as her little body was so frail, so I just leaned over her and stroked the hair on each side of her head, still singing, "Oh, I know a woman named Emily. She is so dear and sweet to me." Her hair was wiry thin. I concentrated on not brushing too hard so as to accidentally stroke her ear. And I was almost startled when Emily's hand came up to cup my wrist.

We just stared at each other. Both our eyes filled with tears and we were both equally swept up in the sweetness of love in the room. I moved my face close to hers and as I rubbed noses with her, said, "I love you too, dearest little Emily."

I sat in the room with her, holding her hand until she fell back to sleep and then left the hospital. I told no one about my day's experience because there simply were no words to explain the miracle moment God had created for us both.

The next Sunday I went back to the hospital to visit Emily once again, but Emily was gone. She had passed on that previous Tuesday. I propped myself up against the same wall, with tears streaming down my cheeks just as before, but this time instead of pleading, I prayed thankfully, "Dear God, thank you for sending Emily to me, for my heart has grown one thousand fold."

I realized that in order to grow spiritually, we must step outside our own little circle in life, to lay our lives down and to be about someone else's life. If we will trust God to move us in the ways He most needs us, then we shall all find the comfort and love of a new friend and find the deepest level of love for God in the secret chambers of our heart.

SIMPLE JOYS

—— Cathy Downs ——

Fields of wildflowers, bluebirds singing,
Chirping crickets, school bells ringing.
Children's laughter, gentle spring breezes,
Soft yellow moonlight, a new baby's sneezes.
Rolling waves at the ocean, hot white sand,
Walks in late evening, couples holding hands.
Fresh mountain water, clear and sweet,
Pink cotton candy, hot chocolate treats.
Strong black coffee, freshly baked bread,
Words of comfort, sincerely said.
Red gingham curtains, polished desks,
Prayers at bedtime, finished tests.
Graded papers, vacation time,
Student poems, perfectly rhymed.
Homemade quilts, shoes that fit,
Color televisions, dogs that sit.
Tangy lemonade, ice cold milk,

Department stores, sales on silk.
Flannel pajamas, interesting books,
Family reunions, pictures that took.
Grandma and Grandpa, birthday dinners,
Blue ribbons on field day, being a winner.
Smiley face stickers, beautiful weather,
Playground swings, families together.
Permanent press, professional cleaners,
Ready-made pizza, low-fat wieners.
Loving parents, a trusting child,
Discipline firm, punishment mild.
Thunder showers, colorful rainbows,
Huge rain puddles, mud between bare toes.
Family albums, no pages blank,
Backyard see-saws made from a plank.
Community baseball, charcoal that burns,
Gentle admonitions, lessons learned.
Sunrises and sunsets, green budding plants,
Soft denim jumpers, elastic waist pants.
Songs of worship, message so clear,
Comfort in knowing God is near.
Forgiveness and compassion, the smile of a child,
Life's simple joys make living worthwhile.

GOD WILL ERASE ALL YOUR FEELINGS OF WORTHLESSNESS

—— Rev. Lawrence D. Pollard ——

There are some people who are successful, and still they are unhappy. They feel rejected, isolated, and worthless. There are other people whose good life turns into disaster because of loss, failure, and sometimes unemployment. There are those who, because of difficulties, have lost their hope; they become despondent. Some people suffer because they have been mistreated, set up, or done in by friends. All of these people lead miserable lives. Yet, people who are miserable can find comfort, relief, peace, and happiness through faith in God. The story of Joseph and his brothers illustrates how Joseph's faith was his strength, courage and comfort in every stage of his life.

Joseph was one of the younger sons of Jacob. Jacob loved him because Joseph was born when Jacob was one year old. Joseph's father was partial to him. Joseph's brothers became envious and jealous of him. Then Joseph would "rat" on them when they were wrong. They hated him for this. Some of the brothers wanted to kill him.

One day, their father sent Joseph into the fields to see his brothers. When they saw him coming, they decided to kill him. One brother did not want to kill Joseph and persuaded his brothers to dig a pit and to put him in it. This they did. Then some merchants from Egypt came by. The brothers took Joseph out of the pit and sold him into slavery to the merchants from Egypt.

Joseph had learned at an early age from his father to have faith in God. In Egypt, Joseph realized that God was with him. His faith moderated his behavior and his attitude. He got a "good job" as a servant in the home of the chief of police. The chief's wife tried to seduce Joseph but had no success. However, she lied to her husband about him. Joseph was then thrown into prison. Again, he realized that God was with him.

One day Pharaoh had a dream and sent for Joseph, who was in prison, to interpret his dream. He was so impressed with Joseph's interpretation that he made Joseph a ruling member of his cabinet. Thus, Joseph saved Egypt from seven years of famine. Joseph was successful. Hence, he offered Thanksgiving to God.

When Joseph's family moved from Canaan, because of the famine there, to Egypt, they did not recognize him. Joseph revealed himself to them and was able, because of faith, to forgive his brothers. They made up and lived in peace.

The lesson that we learned from Joseph is that God is with us each step of the way. If we have faith in God, he will lead us in good time. He will protect us in the time of danger. He will strengthen

14

us when times are difficult. Our faith will temper our behaviors and attitudes. It will not allow us to stay down when we are knocked down. But it will enable us to get up and try again.

Young people can also learn from Joseph. When Joseph was a boy, he learned from his father to have faith in God. As young people grow, like Joseph, God will lead them out of trouble. He will take away their addictions. Instead of joining gangs, they will find wholesome fellowship with young and old who have faith in God. Faith in God will make a difference in our lives.

BEAN STORY

—— Tom Krause ——

Once upon a time there was a bean that lay on the ground. The outer shell of the bean was very hard and solid. The shell protected the inside of the bean from anything on the outside. Time went by and the bean never changed. Never. After a while the bean felt useless and wondered what its purpose was.

One day a farmer passed by and planted the bean in the ground. Rains soon came and, as the water seeped down through the ground and over the bean, the hard shell softened and cracked. The crack allowed the water and nutrients from the soil to enter the inside of the bean. Then a marvelous thing happened. The bean began to grow. A sprout grew from the inside of the bean and, using the water and nutrients from the soil, it began to struggle to work its way to the surface of the ground. As the sprout struggled to reach the surface, it began to grow roots to bring in more water and nutrients for strength. As the sprout finally reached the surface and peeked its head out to the world above, another marvelous event occurred. The light from the sun shone on the sprout causing it to grow faster than before. Finally, the sprout turned into a beautiful plant. The plant then produced many beans of its own that the farmer used to feed many people. Now the bean knew its purpose and never felt useless again.

*AUTHOR'S NOTE: When we open our minds, we begin to grow. When we open our hearts and share our gifts with the world, all mankind benefits. That is when we find our purpose.

IT IS MORE BLESSED TO GIVE
THAN TO RECEIVE

—— Eleanor Hinton ——

When I was a child, I would hear grown-ups say, "It is more blessed to give than to receive." Well, I could not comprehend why it was more blessed to give than to receive. As a child, I often received gifts from family members—particularly at Christmas, Easter, and on my birthday, and it seemed so much more exciting to get those presents than to give them.

As I grew older and more interested in others, I began to comprehend better the meaning of, "It is more blessed to give than to receive." I found myself wanting to give to others without reciprocation.

Sharing and giving are a part of our society. Our society is very benevolent. When we reach out to help others, by giving our time and money to charities, we exemplify the true meaning of, "It is more blessed to give than to receive."

People who give to others, therefore, are blessed. I have always heard, "What you give to others will return to you twofold." I know we do not give in order to receive twofold; we give because within our hearts we want to help others and share with them the blessing we have received from the Almighty.

Not only do we Americans help our own, but international giving is also becoming more prevalent in our country. We see the cry for help on the television as we sit in our comfortable homes, eating. We see children and their parents in foreign countries starving to death from hunger. We willingly make a contribution for the plea to help stop hunger.

As the holiday season approaches, let us continue our generosity and remember that, "It is more blessed to give than to receive." All of us should share our time and generosity with those who are less fortunate. That is the true meaning of Christmas, and Christmas contains a sense of giving, meant to be celebrated everyday.

REMEMBER TO REMEMBER—
YOUR LIFE IS YOUR MESSAGE

—— D. Trinidad Hunt ——

We are invited guests
In the garden of God

Cultivate your character
As a gardener
Cultivates his garden

First loosen the soil
In the mind
By releasing old habits
And attitudes
That no longer serve you
Then choose wisely
The new seed you wish
To plant in this freshly
Turned soil

Finally, water and nurture
The seed by doing your
Best each day
And as one day dissolves
And spills
Into the next
The harvest of your life
Will yield a new crop

Weed out your weaknesses
And develop your strengths

For a master
Is one
Who was
Mastered himself

LILLY

—— *Cathy Downs* ——

Slowly, methodically, and painfully, Lilly worked her arthritic fingers around the tiny pearl buttons on the front of her delicate white blouse. Twice already she had fastened the buttons in the wrong holes. She forced herself to slow her movements in order that she not make that mistake again. Being so excited made her clumsy, but it was Sunday! Lilly's children and grandchildren would be visiting her today!

Every Sunday, Lilly laid out her very best outfit to wear, the only outfit she kept for special company—her white lace blouse with tiny pearl buttons and her long black taffeta skirt that covered her wasted withered legs which were usually so obvious in the wheelchair.

Before her husband died ten years ago, this outfit was the one he loved to see Lilly wear. His eyes always sparkled with delight when she dressed up in her special blouse and skirt. Ten years seemed like such an eternity. Five of those ten years had found Lilly confined to a wheelchair, totally disabled by arthritis, but she had never gotten used to sitting all day.

Although the motion was excruciatingly painful for Lilly, she forced her arms upward and brushed and plaited her fine silver hair into a long neat braid. She wound the braid around the top of her head into a tight coronet. To hold the braid in place, she inserted a lovely antique comb. This comb had been given to her on Mother's Day several years ago by her only daughter. When her daughter came to see her today, she would be pleased to see that Lilly still had the comb and that she wore it in her hair. She saved the comb for special occasions—special occasions and Sundays.

Wearing any kind of shoes hurt Lilly's tender crooked feet, but she didn't want to wear her ugly brown bedroom shoes with her Sunday outfit. She slipped the black, shiny patent leather flats onto her stiff feet. She knew her children would comment on the pretty way she looked, fussing at her for going to all that trouble especially for their visit.

Next, Lilly opened the top drawer in the dresser beside her bed and removed a delicately framed picture of her son, his wife, and their two children. Such a lovely family! Lilly never displayed the picture during the week, afraid that she would accidentally knock it to the floor and break it, reaching for something on the dresser. Sometimes she was so clumsy.

Proudly, Lilly placed the picture beside the faded yellow silk daffodils that her grandchildren had given her many Easters ago. She just couldn't bear to throw them out; the memory of them was too special to her.

As difficult as it was to accomplish, Lilly applied pressed powder and rose-colored rouge to her face. Her eyes weren't strong anymore and she had trouble focusing as she looked in the mirror. Lilly guessed it was better that her children didn't write her a lot of letters, since her tired old eyes really had trouble making out print these days. Applying her rouge carefully, she hoped that she hadn't painted the red circles on her cheeks too heavily. Her son hated that. He usually made her wash her face.

Satisfied with her appearance, Lilly wheeled herself over to the window and drew back the curtains. She wanted to see her grandchildren as they got out of the car to come inside. That first glimpse of them was so special.

What a beautiful Lord's Day! As she looked out the window, Lilly longed to be outside. How wonderful it would be to feel the fresh spring breeze on her face, to enjoy the warm morning sun on her back, to smell the freshly blooming flowers, to touch the coolness of the dewy grass with her bare feet. Maybe her son would take her outside for a little while today. She did so love to watch her grandchildren run and play.

Warm from the sun filtering through the window, Lilly dozed, exhausted from the morning's chore of getting ready for her Sunday visit with her children.

When Lilly awoke, several hours later, she shivered from the chill in the air. The sun had gone down outside and twilight had come. Lilly's back and legs ached horribly from hours of sitting and waiting in her wheelchair. She could feel the swelling in her feet from wearing the tight-fitting Sunday shoes. Her head ached from having her hair wound so tightly. The comb pressed painfully into her skull, leaving an imprint on her scalp.

Lilly strained to see the digital numbers on the bedside clock across the room. Realizing the lateness of the hour, Lilly turned her wheelchair around and positioned herself beside her bed. She was so tired. So old. Where had the years gone so quickly?

Slowly Lilly removed her patent shoes and placed them carefully back under the bed in their original box. With tired aching fingers she struggled to unfasten the tiny pearl buttons on her blouse. Lilly folded the blouse lovingly, as she did with her black taffeta skirt. She placed the garments gently into a yellowed cardboard box and closed the lid tenderly. With a crumpled tissue, she cleaned off the pressed powder and rouge, easy to remove now because of the wet streaks left by her tears of disappointment.

After donning her worn flannel nightgown with much difficulty, Lilly raised herself to the edge of the bed, slid out of her wheelchair and struggled under the covers. "They'll come next Sunday," she whispered to herself. "I know they will. They won't forget."

In the hall outside, the night shift nurse at The Families' Choice Nursing Home passed room 132, looked in on Lilly, and sadly shook her head. Quietly she reached inside the room and turned out the light.

A REFLECTION ON MY BAPTISM

—— Eleanor Hinton ——

On a January Sunday I witnessed a baptism at my church. I had not witnessed a baptism like this in quite some time. On this particular Sunday, something very sacred and unusual hung in the air of the church.

I had gone to church earlier that morning to present a donation to my minister for the Sunday School. I had not planned to remain for the church service. After giving my minister the donation, I lingered around the church, talking to members as they came in. There were others arriving in preparation for today's service.

At this point, I felt a compelling force as if guided by an angel, telling me not to leave as I had planned. Finally, one church member said to me, "It is 10:20; you might as well stay for church." It did not take much to encourage me to stay because I had heard an angel's heavenly voice whispering to me to remain at church.

Since I had not eaten breakfast, I told the church member I would leave and return. And I did just that. When I returned and entered the sanctuary, I was given a program for the order of service. I took my seat in the back of the church in the last pew, as

I sometimes do. While reading the program, I looked up and saw the choir march in and sit on the left side of the church. I realized we would be participating in a baptism today. As the choir took their places, I looked to the front of the church and noticed the mirror behind the pulpit.

"A Baptism!" I said to myself. In the mirror I saw the reflection of water in a kind of pool. Then I saw my minister, dressed in white, descend the steps into the water. As he stood in the water, a pre-teen walked toward him, also draped in white. One by one, other youngsters approached the pool to be dipped. All of them were dressed in white, and deacons assisted them to the pool for their confession and acceptance of Christ. Family members and friends craned their necks to see their loved ones being baptized. One father took pictures when his children entered the pool.

As the youths were dipped, I started to reminisce about my own baptism and all my fear and joy that week following my acceptance of Christ. The Sunday I decided to be a witness for Christ was the beginning of a weeklong revival service. My grandmother had discussed with me what it meant to be a Christian. I was eleven years old and thought it was time to surrender my all to Him. I remember crying on that Sunday when I stood up. Grandmother was there to give me her hand as I took my shaking steps to the front of the church. The minister went through the regular Baptist procedure for someone wanting to surrender to Christ. I had to sit on the mourners' bench with others who had or would be surrendering to Christ that revival week. The mourners' bench was the first pew in the sanctuary. Everyone knew those sitting there were making a giant step.

Baptism for me was a giant step. I was a little afraid but I was thrilled because this was the day I would take my dip in the creek not far from the church. To me, being a Christian meant living by the Ten Commandments, as best as an eleven-year-old could. And to me, being baptized was the final step of the cleansing process for being a Christian. Grandmother draped a white sheet around me for the baptism, and I felt like an angel. I could hear the singing and clapping and people making a joyful noise unto the Lord. The church members eagerly waited for the minister to start the baptizing. All who had sat on the mourners' bench for the week would walk into the creek and be dipped. Yes, I was afraid of the water, but I knew I had to be dipped.

As I left my memory, I returned to witnessing the baptism. I thought about how things had changed since I was baptized in the creek. I said to myself, "Grandmother would be so surprised to see how things are done now."

After baptizing the children, the minister finally came to the pulpit in his robe to preach the sermon of the day. I thought the sermon "An Antidote for Fear" was very appropriate. *Fear* is the word! I thought to myself. I wondered how the young people felt about being Christians and if they had feared, as I had, being dipped under the water. The minister stated in the sermon, "God is with you. You need not fear. He will not abandon you. You should build your hopes on things eternal and hold to God's unchanging hands."

As I listened to the sermon, I thought, "What a beautiful message for a Sunday baptizing!" So moved was I by the service and by my own memories of surrendering to Christ, that I thought about it for days. Finally, my curiosity got the best of me and I was compelled again to go back into the church. This time the sanctuary was empty and I walked alone past the pews to the empty pool to take a good look at the symbol of newness and change.

THANK YOU FAMILY...

—— James Malinchak ——

Thank you family…

For teaching me wrong from right
    And encouraging me to keep my dreams in sight,

For showing me not to let obstacles keep me down
    And for creating a smile from my frown,

For saying that you care about me
    And for showing just how special love should be,

For wiping my tears away when I'm feeling sad
    And for calming me down when I tend to get mad,

For helping others with the good that you do
    And for teaching me that I should help others, too,

For hugging me when I am feeling blue
　　And whispering into my ear "I love you,"

Thank you, family, for all that you do
　　I don't know where I would be if it weren't for you.

I AM...

—— Amy Yerkes ——

I am an architect: I've built a solid foundation and each year I go to school I add another floor of wisdom and knowledge.

I am a sculptor: I've shaped my morals and philosophies according to the clay of right and wrong.

I am a painter: With each new idea I express, I paint a new hue in the world's multitude of colors.

I am a scientist: Each day that passes by, I gather new data, make important observations, and experiment with new concepts and ideas.

I am an astrologist: Reading and analyzing the palms of life and each new person I encounter.

I am an astronaut: Constantly exploring and broadening my horizons.

I am a doctor: I heal those who turn to me for consultation and advice, and I bring out the vitality in those people who seem lifeless.

I am a lawyer: I'm not afraid to stand up for my basic rights, and those of all others.

I am a police officer: I always watch out for others' welfare and I am always on the scene preventing fights and keeping the peace.

I am a teacher: By my example others learn the importance of determination, dedication, and hard work.

I am a mathematician: Making sure I conquer each one of my problems with correct solutions.

I am a detective: Peering through my two lenses, searching for meaning and significance in the mysteries of life.

I am a juror: Judging others and their situations only after I've heard and understood the entire story.

I am a banker: Others share their trust and values with me and never lose interest.

I am a hockey player: Watching out for and dodging those who try to block my goal.

I am a marathon runner: Full of energy, always moving, and ready for the next challenge.

I am a mountain climber: Slowly but surely I am making my way to the top.

I am a tight-rope walker: Carefully and stealthily I pace myself through every rough time, but I always make it safely to the end.

I am a millionaire: Rich in love, sincerity, and compassion, and I own a wealth of knowledge, wisdom, experience, and insight, which is priceless.

Most importantly, I am me.

MY FAITH IN GOD

—— Eleanor Hinton ——

"My Faith in God" was previously published
in *Waiting for a Miracle* by Eleanor Hinton.

*This story is an affirmation of my faith in God in raising a mentally
challenged son.*

There are times when I wonder, "Why me Lord? Why
me?" However, I know God only gives you what you can bear.
Sometimes the cross gets very heavy, but you must continue the
journey. There are periods of time when I must pray more for K.P.,
so I burn a candle every night for thirty days and pray during the
middle of the night for him. It seems as though my prayers are
better heard in the stillness of the night. My experience with K.P.
has been a test of faith.

One night, I received a call from the nurse at the agency for the
group home. K.P. had been taken to the hospital for pushing his
hand through the windowpane in his bedroom. I was hysterical. I
did not know what to do. I threatened to sue the agency for letting

this happen. Not being able to visit K.P. made things worse. He was not receptive to visits from family unless we were taking him home. Our presence would make it worse for the staff to handle him. (He always wants to come home, and whenever he sees me, he thinks he is going home.) I prayed to God he would not have a serious injury. I couldn't sleep until I heard from the hospital. Finally, I was told that he received ten stitches and had been seen by a psychiatrist. He was released back to the group home. How frightening this must have been for him. I was happy that the injury wasn't any worse.

Where does one get the resiliency to keep going? From Almighty God, who continues to give me strength.

Often I felt as if I couldn't go on. Where could I turn? The only emotional support I had came from my middle son, my support group, and some friends who were very close to me. My husband, at that time, was not supportive, psychologically or emotionally. I thought, dear Lord, just put someone in my life who understands what I am going through.

Although God grants us the opportunity to parent and rear children to the age of reason, there are some he leaves with us for a lifetime—perpetual children to have and comfort perhaps for reasons only he knows. So we give them our love, and, most often, the love they give us back is pure and childlike, even after they are "adults." When K.P. is at his best, he gives pure love… and it is truly cherished.

THE MIRACLE CAT

—— Fran Capo ——

This is not your typical nine lives tale. It's about a cat that I found fifteen years ago wrapped in an old flannel shirt in a snow bank outside of a supermarket. Its eyes weren't even open yet and it had to be fed with an eyedropper. The kitten was so tiny that I couldn't distinguish whether it was male or female, so I named it Bonnie. Turns out I was wrong. Bonnie was a he.

Bonnie was very mischievous, just the way I like my animals, full of life and curiosity. He was a Sylvester look alike, without the attitude. Bon, as I called him for short, and I formed a bond. He used to play hide and seek with me, share my peanut butter sandwiches and purr so loudly that he could give a lawn mower a run for its money.

Bonnie was a true ambassador. I could bring any species of animal into the house and Bonnie would immediately take to it, from birds to rabbits to turtles and dogs. He never once in fifteen years hissed or ran. He coolly would check out the visitor and then go on his merry way. Nothing seemed to bother Bon. He was eternally happy and always purring.

And this is how life was with Bon until one day when I returned from my honeymoon. Bonnie wasn't there to greet me. I thought maybe he was angry I had been away for a week. I searched the house calling for him. No answer. Not that I was expecting a, "Hey, where have you been?" but this was very un-Bon-like. Then I found him under the bed, lying in a pool of blood and urine, with pupils dilated as big as hubcaps.

I gently called his name. He forced out a weak meow saying, "Help me." I looked in his eyes and could see his pain. I rolled back the bed and picked him up and took him to the twenty-four hour emergency clinic. I was told he was dehydrated and had kidney stones. That his passage had gotten blocked by these stones, and finally they burst and all the blood and urine came gushing out. The doctors stuck in tubes to open up and clear up the passage. He was kept over night to re-hydrate.

The next day Bon seemed to be back to his old self. Then two nights later it happened again. Again I rushed him to the emergency hospital. The procedure was the same. The next day I took him to the vet. Bonnie was seven at the time. He had only been to a vet when he was a kitten. He had never been sick. The vet told me he needed a low ash diet, that this blockage is common in male cats. The vet cleaned him out and told me to observe him; if it persisted, we would have to operate.

By this time, my then husband, who wasn't too fond of animals, was calling him the million-dollar cat. The vet bills were pretty high, over the $1,000 mark already. My husband even suggested that, if it persisted, I should just put the cat to sleep. After all, it was "just an alley cat."

Animals can become part of your life. Your soul bonds with theirs. You communicate on a whole different level with them, almost spiritually. Anyway, my husband slept on the couch for a few nights for those remarks.

A few more days and the incident occurred again. The vet told me we would have to operate. I told him to do whatever was necessary to have Bonnie back and pain free. He told me it was the only way. First, however, Bonnie had to take a feline leukemia test. If the results came back positive, we'd be in real trouble. He had to have the operation to live, but if he had leukemia, once they opened him up for surgery, Bonnie would immediately die. The oxygen hitting his system would kick in and the leukemia would spread.

They took the test and the results were sent to the lab. The following day I received the grave news. "Bonnie has leukemia. There is no choice but to put him to sleep. We cannot operate." I was in shock. I asked the vet if it was possible that the lab had made a mistake. He said, "Highly unlikely. We do hundreds of these tests and haven't had a mistake yet. I know this is hard. It's best to do it soon before the cat is in any more pain. Think of Bonnie."

A million thoughts raced through my head. "Don't be in denial." "Do what's right for Bonnie." But then another thought came into my mind, "nothing is impossible." I told the doctor

I wanted one more day before I put Bonnie to sleep. In the meantime, I didn't care the cost, I wanted the test retaken. I kissed Bonnie on the head and whispered. "Don't worry." I'm not sure if that was said more for him or me.

That night I went home strangely calm. All my life I believed that nothing was impossible. I believed that believing is seeing. If you focus, have unyielding faith, strongly visualize positive results, and really believe in them, the subconscious mind will manifest them. I spent three hours that night acting as if Bonnie was okay. I felt in my whole being that he was cured. Then I visualized the vet saying, "I can't believe this, the lab made a mistake. We can operate and Bonnie will be fine." I kept picturing that scene over and over again as if it had already happened. Then I thanked God for the miracle and went to sleep.

The next day I went to the vet. He said, "Sit down, you are not going to believe this." But I already knew. The vet swore it had never happened before. He operated on Bonnie, and Bonnie is alive and purring as I write.

But, it doesn't end there. Bonnie is now a card-carrying senior citizen, about 135 to you and me. A few months ago Bonnie had an infection and his face ballooned up. He had to stay three days at a vet, a different vet. The operation on his face left a gaping wound, the size of a dime, and so deep that you could see the mouth muscles moving. Bonnie was also diagnosed as diabetic.

He needed insulin shots. I couldn't afford it. So I was told he had a few months to live. He was an old cat, deaf now.

Again, I went home and prayed and visualized. Within a week, Bonnie's face healed completely, he gained weight, and acted very perky. The vet said it was amazing. He had given me a grave diagnosis, and even though Bon still has diabetes, he looks very healthy. He said, "Sometimes you just don't know with these things. Bonnie has a strong will."

To me it was another miracle. But, was it really a miracle? Or just unexpected positive results? Bonnie, my miracle cat, just keeps shocking them. I know eventually Bonnie will leave this earth, but for now the cat purrs on with seven lives left to go.

DOT EVERY "I" AND CROSS EVERY "T"

—— Eleanor Hinton ——

My Granddad's favorite expression was "you must dot every 'i' and cross every 't' in life." When I was young, I thought this expression was nonsense. I would say to myself, "You do that anyway. What is he talking about? Everyone dots their 'i's and crosses their 't's. That's what good penmanship is!"

I was too young to understand that Granddad's expression was metaphorical, that he was not talking about good penmanship. It wasn't until years later that I realized the depth of Granddad's favorite expression. I overheard a professor using the expression to emphasize the importance of being careful to follow the rules and do the right thing.

Granddad has been deceased for thirty years now, and, in those thirty years, I have heard myself using his expression countless times. It reminds me to take care of details and mind the given rules of a situation. In a small way, this little "nonsense" expression has had a tremendous impact on my life.

Just the other day I was visiting a school, and I heard the teacher telling the principal that she was going to make certain to dot all 'i's and cross all 't's. I knew that the principal understood this metaphor, but I wondered if students would think the expression meant that they had to work harder on their penmanship. Whatever the case, I thought, the expression might stick with them, as it did with me and help them to make their lives as fulfilling as mine. Living by this simple expression has helped me steer clear of many potential problems in life.

Now, Granddad had a favorite addendum to his simple expression. He would end the conversation by saying, "You must dot every 'i' and cross every 't'—if you don't you will be a lost ball in high weeds." You can imagine what this new metaphor did to my literal brain. Well, many years have passed since Granddad confused me with his strange expressions, but I still find myself thinking of and using them. And I've managed to stay out of high weeds.

THE WOMAN

—— Jessica Magers ——

Alone
    But not lonely
Aggressive
    But not hostile

The woman reaches out
    With fist open
        To hold another's hand
The woman reaches out
    To comfort another's grief
The woman reaches out
    To laugh joyfully with another in happiness

The woman reaches up
    With fist clenched
    With head raised
        In her demand

            for power
            for rights
            for equality

She has endured the pain
        of hatred
        of spite
        of inequality
For centuries
From her mouth she quotes
    "And still I rise, I rise, I rise"

The woman lives in us
    All
She struggles to be heard
    In some
In others, she is as free as a bird,
    Singing sweetly

But whatever her status in each of us
    There is only one thing
That she is
    To all of us

        Beautiful

IF ADULTS ONLY UNDERSTOOD...

—— *Jason Summey* ——

Over the past two years I have spent a lot of time developing and setting up the "Be Cool....Stay in School" program. During this time, I have given many speeches, been featured several times on national television and radio, written a book about the program and contributed a story that appeared in the book *Chicken Soup for the Teenage Soul.*

When I started, I didn't realize that all this exposure would result in teenagers all over the world writing to me. Nearly all of these letters congratulated me on my efforts to keep kids in school, but most of them went on to ask me for advice. In fact, there were so many, I began to feel like an advice columnist.

Kids from Singapore to Spain, from Canada to Grenada, have written about one common problem. They feel no one cares! They feel parents don't care, teachers don't care, and friends don't care. They write asking how to get people to care more about each other. Well, I don't have any proven solutions, but I do have some thoughts.

I think there is a common reason why teenagers rebel and sometimes act mean toward adults and even each other. The reason is that people are so busy looking for what's wrong with other people that they can't find the good in them. As a result, the world is filled with people who treat other people badly. In several letters, teenagers complain that their school feels more like a prison than a place to learn. They feel teachers are more interested in looking for something to punish than something to reward. Others say they dread being at home. They feel their parents just want to find fault and criticize everything that they do.

We probably can't change negative people, but we can change the way we act around them. We can give them a sincere smile before they have a chance to say anything. Have you ever noticed it's harder to be mean to someone with a smile on their face than someone with a scowl? We can pay them a genuine compliment before they have a chance to say something ugly. It's difficult to be ugly to someone who has just said something nice about you. We can also honestly offer our help. It's tough to criticize someone who you feel really wants to help you.

Wouldn't it be great if parents only understood that teenagers would be better teenagers if they were greeted with a smile, paid a compliment and offered support? And wouldn't school be more fun if teachers just realized that students would be better students if they were greeted with a smile, paid a compliment, and offered support?

Why do people have to be so mean? Why can't the world be a better place? Why can't parents be better parents and teachers be better teachers? Maybe we can't change negative people, but if we teenagers greet them with a smile, pay them a compliment, and offer our support, who knows what might happen? The world may even start to become a better place, especially if we are patient and give positive actions time to work. Oh, if adults only understood…

THE LEADER

—— *Tony Overman* ——

If only they knew how hard it is for me.
In turning sixteen, the world I begin to see.

My friends begin to change, right before my eyes,
and now they seem to laugh, and tell all sorts of lies.

They hang around together in groups of three or four;
The language they use...it isn't gentle anymore.

Somehow I feel rejected, because I don't conform.
Those that step to their own beat don't seem to be the norm.

I've watched a few just fade away to drugs and alcohol;
and many more have given up...too many to recall.

Alcohol is an option for everyone in my school.
I've lost a friend to booze again. I will not be a fool.

And sex, it seems so open for everyone to explore.
Three girls I knew who came to school don't come anymore.

If I could make a difference, what could I do or say?
I would go to school, try my best each and every day.

There is one thing I'd like to do before I graduate...
I'd like to touch them one by one before it is to late.

THE BUMBLEBEE DRILL

—— *Tom Krause* ——

As she sat in my first hour health class the beginning of her sophomore year in high school, Crystal appeared to be just another anonymous face that blended into a sea of new faces that started each new semester. She didn't really seem to fit into any of the popular cliques, but she had a caring quality about her that made people feel comfortable around her. There always did, however, seem to be something empty or missing, evident from the way she would sometimes stare out the window.

One Friday I decided to break up the monotony of class by doing an activity I call the bumblebee drill. The students all selected a partner and arranged their chairs in a circle in the middle of the room. One of the partners began by sitting in a chair while the other partner stood behind them. I explained that the students who were standing were the bees and the students who were sitting were the flowers. I went on to explain that I would play a CD of soft music and while the music was playing it was the job of the bees to nurture the flowers by giving them a gentle neck and shoulder massage. Every minute I would say switch and the

51

bees would have to go to another flower for nurturing. We would continue until all the bees nurtured all the flowers. Then we would trade places and let the bees become the flowers and the flowers become the bees. The students loved it.

Things were going fine until a student came up to me and said, "Coach, Crystal is crying!"

I went over to Crystal and asked her if she needed help. She explained to me that, two days before her eighth birthday, her mother died. The song that was playing was her mother's favorite song. "Coach," she said, "I miss my mom."

As I held her, you could have heard a pin drop. By now everyone was concerned for Crystal. I asked her if any of her classmates knew this story and she said it was something she just kept inside herself. I asked her to share the story with her classmates, and she did. I told the class we were going to play the song again and that, if they wanted to, they could come up and stand next to Crystal as she remembered her mother. As soon as the music began all the students came up and stood by their friend. Some cried with her, some hugged her, some just placed their hand on her shoulder. It was very moving.

When the song was over everyone dried their eyes and went back to their seats. Crystal turned to her classmates and said, "Thank you—I feel like I have a lot of friends."

She was never just an anonymous face again. She had lots of friends, including me, and the smile she wore from then on proved it.

AN INVITATION TO LATANYA

—— Nailah Malik ——

LaTanya Gaston was a young lady of considerable promise. With finesse she held down a fifteen-hour-a-week job at the library and was a full-time high school student. Not only was she a good worker, her excellence in academics earned her a college scholarship. During the summer before her first year of college, a new development unfolded in LaTanya's life. Into her life entered a young man. Not that this was a first, mind you. Over the course of her high school years there had been friendships with other guys, but none were quite so serious as this one seemed.

This young man played the relationship game close to the cuff. He accompanied LaTanya to the library every day. Once there, he remained the entire time she was working. He took a seat in that portion of the reading area that afforded an eagle's eye view of LaTanya's workstation, and the little amount of time he did not spend eyeballing LaTanya, he spent browsing through teen magazines.

He made no overtures of friendliness to any of the library staff members. Two weeks after his first appearance, a circulation desk worker tried to penetrate the wall of silence by inviting the young man to apply for a library card and check out books. He reciprocated this friendly gesture with a cold and flat, "No, thanks."

Often this young man took a break from his watch post, but he never left the library for more than an hour. He always returned in time to escort LaTanya home at the end of her work shift.

Soon LaTanya's remarks and body language transmitted a message of discontent to fellow workers. Scattered comments made here and there about her new boyfriend let us know her boyfriend was loaded with personal deficits. He posed an annoyance and embarrassment by insisting on coming to work with her every day. He was overbearing and crowded her space. He held no regard for her feelings.

For the longest time her resentment was withheld from the boyfriend. Finally, LaTanya mustered enough courage to have a frank talk with him about his undesirable behavior. The first time LaTanya discussed this problem with the young man, he made no comment at all. He simply ignored her (a method of control known as passive aggression). After noticing no change in his behavior, LaTanya tried talking with him a second time. This initiative produced horrible results. The lid flew off the boiling kettle as he went into a rage and accused her of attempting to be unfaithful (a controlling strategy that shifts blame for discomfort to the victim). Though disappointed and a bit bewildered by his reaction, from that point on, for the sake of keeping peace, LaTanya steered clear of this volatile subject.

For more than two months this uncomfortable situation persisted. LaTanya's anxiety and frustration became increasingly visible. The intrusion into her space and privacy added a coating of gloom and despair to what had before been her outgoing and sunshiny personality.

One day LaTanya came to work without her bodyguard. The same thing happened over the next three days. On the fifth day of work, while sorting our books for re-shelving, LaTanya opened up to a co-worker. The true nature of her relationship was exposed. She explained that, for the longest time, Marcus had been pushing her to do something she did not want to do.

"He wanted me to have his baby," said LaTanya. "Like Tamika, Kiesha, and Shawnda, had done for Rashaud and them. He was trying to get me to have a baby so that I would qualify to go on welfare. He wanted me to get on welfare and give him the money I would then receive." After pausing momentarily as if to take in a badly needed inhalation of air, she forged on. "I finally convinced him I was not willing to do this. So he broke up with me and found some other girl who promised that she would do this for him."

Soon after this revelation, the old LaTanya was restored. She was rejuvenated, filled to the brim with enthusiasm. With the proper perspective firmly intact, she glided forward, preparing for entrance to college that fall. Given that she had already passed such a formidable exam with Marcus, success in college was almost certain. Moreover, the direction in which she was now going was the result of having made a life choice.

As for Marcus and his new girlfriend, they too had made choices that would change the course of their lives. Unfortunately, they chose to become ensnared in the welfare trap. Even though evidence abounds that this option rewards its beneficiaries with a stress-ridden existence of hardship and disappointment, incredibly, there are still those who succumb to this magnetic field of human waste. There are those who, of free accord and by choice, venture into this wasteland where assuredly a heap of sorrow, despair, and hopelessness lie in wait.

The common denominator of these parties in the above-described case study is that each was presented an opportunity to make a choice for themselves. The choices that were made are tantamount to a person seeking water from a well. One arrived carrying a sturdy metal bucket, while the other two arrived carrying a bucket riddled with holes in the bottom. How one withdraws water from the well is completely up to the individual. In a universe of possibilities, it all boils down to a matter of self-esteem.

SEE ME

—— Lisa Helms-Constant ——

Look past my appearance,
For my smile is but a decoy.
The twinkle in my eye is forced.
My attentiveness wanders,
Yet my conscience brings me back.
I tremble inside with fear,
Though my frame is strong and sturdy.
The truth is what I long for,
Yet I settle for a broken heart.
My dreams have become a blur,
Though I cling to hope with all my being.
Tears fall from my eyes,
Though privacy is my code of honor.
See me for what I am,
Not who you want me to be.
Love me if you want to,
Not because you feel you must.

Long for me with your heart,
Do not long for me as a convenience.
Alas, I ask,
See me.

A BROTHER'S VOICE

—— *James Malinchak* ——

Most people experience inspiration in their lives. Maybe it's a talk with someone you respect or an experience that you had. Whatever the inspiration, it tends to make you look at life from a different perspective. My inspiration came from my sister, Vicki, a kind and caring person. She didn't care about accolades or being written about in newspapers. All she wanted was to share her love with the people she cared about, her family and friends.

The summer before my junior year of college, I received a phone call from my father, saying that Vicki had been rushed to the hospital. She had collapsed and the right side of her body was paralyzed. The preliminary indications were that she had suffered a stroke. However, test results confirmed it was much more serious. There was a malignant brain tumor causing her paralysis. Her doctors didn't give her more than three months to live.

I remember wondering how this could happen? The day before, Vicki had been perfectly fine. Now, her life was coming to an end at such a young age.

After overcoming the initial shock and feeling of emptiness, I decided that Vicki needed hope and encouragement. She needed someone to make her believe that she would overcome this obstacle. I became Vicki's coach. Everyday we would visualize the tumor shrinking and everything that we talked about was positive. I even posted a sign on her hospital room door that read, "If you have any negative thoughts, leave them at the door."

I was determined to help Vicki beat the tumor. She and I made a deal that we called fifty-fifty. I would do fifty percent of the fighting and Vicki would do the other fifty percent.

The month of August arrived and it was time to begin my junior year of college three thousand miles away. I was unsure whether I should leave or stay with Vicki. I made the mistake of telling her that I might not leave for school. She became angry and said not to worry because she would be fine. There was Vicki lying ill in a hospital bed telling me not to worry. I realized that if I stayed, it might send a message that she was dying and I didn't want her believing that. Vicki needed to believe that she could win against the tumor.

Leaving that night, feeling it might be the last time I would ever see Vicki alive, was the most difficult thing I have ever done. While at school, I never stopped fighting my fifty percent for her. Every night before falling asleep I would talk to Vicki, hoping that there was some way she could hear me. I would say, "Vicki, I'm fighting for you and I will never quit. As long as you never quit fighting, we will beat this."

A few months passed and she still held on. I was talking with an elderly friend and she asked about Vicki's situation. I told her that she was getting worse but that she wasn't quitting. My friend asked a question that really made me think. She said, "Do you think the reason she hasn't let go is because she doesn't want to let you down?"

Maybe she was right? Maybe I was selfish for encouraging Vicki to keep fighting? That night before falling asleep, I said to her, "Vicki, I understand that you're in a lot of pain and that you might like to let go. If you do, then I want you to. We didn't lose because you never quit fighting. If you want to go on to a better place then I understand. We will be together again. I love you and I'll always be with you wherever you are."

Early the next morning, my mother called to tell me that Vicki had passed away.

MATTERS OF THE HEART

—— Lisa Helms-Constant ——

A pot of gold awaits you at the end of a rainbow mist
Filled with dreams and passions, that no one can resist
Consisting of gems and rubies, surrounded by a sweet vanilla kiss
With diamonds blinding your senses that you can only see
    through the mist

To reach the end of the rainbow you must cross the waterfall
With cascades of beaded jewels splashing against the mountain's
    wall
Step ever so lightly as you cross the path of hope
For this is the place where dreams are built and people are
    nursed to cope

Try not to take the easy way out and hop on a unicorn's back
Try not to forget your focus, lose your balance, and get off track
Although it may seem miles away, there is a reason you are here
Focus on your dreams and passions, try to let go of the fear

The treasure at the end of the rainbow cannot be opened by wishes
It cannot be opened by materialism handed out on golden dishes
You must endure life's experiences and take responsibility for
    your part
For the way to reach the pot of gold, is through matters of the heart.

WOULD YOU ENJOY THE CASCADES OF LIFE

—— *Lisa Helms-Constant* ——

What if you could see where a drop of water began
And where it ended?
Would you tame it to become a waterfall?
Would you let it run wild with other rainfall?
Would you let the mass turn into whitecapped currents,
Or would you try to stifle what is going to be?

Would you welcome the breathtaking sight of wild green
Surrounding a cascade of waterfall, or would you mock
The fact that everything is out of place, not trimmed or neat!
If the sun beat down a scorching energy upon your face,
Would you endure the heat or make a play for a cool stream?

Simplicity is where the drop of water begins and
Complication is where it ends!
Life for some may be more complicated than others
But for those whose truth this holds,
They have been given spiritual strength!

Waterfalls are like life, as we have choices
We can choose togetherness, simplicity, and love
For if it were not for all of the drops of water coming together
There would be no waterfall at all!!!

BRIGHTLY BURNS THE FLAME

—— *Tom Krause* ——

* Poem for a lost loved one

When I hear your name, the feeling's still the same.
Brightly burns the flame that you gave to me.
Deep within my soul your love is still aglow.
I can't let it go—it's such a part of me.

Memories that we had of good times and sad
make me feel so glad that our love was true.
You left so long ago, still I think you know
that with each day I grow all because of you.

From somewhere in the night comes this shining light.
And it burns so bright—I want to hold on tight.
Maybe it's a sign from deep within my mind
of a love I left behind or one I've yet to find.

Maybe now I see what you did for me.
You gave unselfishly then you set me free.
Now when I hear your name, the feeling's still the same.
Brightly burns the flame that you gave to me.

A CALL FOR SUBMISSIONS

Brunswick Stew 2 Every person has a story to tell or a poem in his or her heart. The writings included in this anthology were written by people just like you. If you have a story to share that can help people make it through the day, or poetic words to inspire us in difficult time, please submit them for consideration for publication in *Brunswick Stew 2*, and ask a friend or family member to submit too. The more we all think about, write and read uplifting thoughts, the more peace we all gain.

Mail submissions to:
Eleanor Hinton
Brunswick Stew 2
P.O. Box 2505
Landover Hills, MD 20784

ABOUT THE EDITOR

Eleanor Hinton, the author of *Waiting for a Miracle,* is a freelance writer, motivational speaker, and consultant.

Eleanor is the editor and publisher of the *National Conference for Substitute Teachers, Inc. Newsletter*. She has also published a *Handbook for Substitute Teachers*, and other materials such as *Self-Esteem and the Substitute,* and *Classroom Management for the Substitutes.* She speaks regularly to substitute teachers at conferences across the nation.

The editor is a retired guidance counselor and holds a master's degree, plus sixty additional credits in guidance and counseling. She is also the mother of three sons and is known for her sense of humor and down-to-earth style.

Eleanor lives in Springdale, Maryland.

CONTRIBUTORS

Fran Capo is a stand-up comic, author of three books, lecturer, and *Guinness Book of World Records* Fastest Talking Female. She has appeared on over eighty-seven television shows, including the "Rosie O'Donnell Show" and "Entertainment Tonight." She is the mother of the world's youngest comic and Bonnie's best friend. She may be reached at: P.O. Box 580272, Flushing, NY 11358.

Lisa Helms-Constant enjoys writing poetry. She plans to publish a book of poems soon. She may be reached at: 430 South Pine Street, Richmond, VA 23220.

Cathy Downs is a Reading Specialist at East Burke Middle School in Burke County, North Carolina. Her hobbies are writing, singing, and reading. Currently, she is working on a children's novel which should be completed in the near future. Cathy has been published in *The Reading Teacher, Guideposts,* and *Chicken Soup for the Woman's Soul.* Correspondence may be sent to: Cathy Downs, P.O. Box 1231, Valdese, NC 28690.

D. Trinidad Hunt is an international author, educator, speaker, corporate trainer/consultant, and co-founder of the Elan Learning Institute and World Youth Network International. Her award-winning book, *Learning to Learn: Maximizing your Performance Potential,* and audiocassette series have propelled numerous companies to organizational excellence. Trin's latest book, *The Operator's Manual for Planet Earth - An Adventure for the Soul,* was released in September 1996 by Hyperion Press and is a Book of the Month Club selection. For further information on training, public speaking, and products, call 800-707-ELAN, fax 808-239-2482, or write to Elan Enterprises at 47-430 Hui Nene Street, Kaneohe, HI 96744.

Tom Krause has taught in the Missouri Public School system for twenty years. He obtained an M.S. in Education in 1968. Tom is a published poet and songwriter most noted for his poem, *Just Me,* in the NY Times Bestseller, *Chicken Soup for the Teenage Soul.* Tom also speaks to thousands of people each year as a motivational speaker for Positive People Presentations, which he started. He speaks at school assemblies and workshops, as well as state and national conventions for schools and businesses. Tom may be reached at the 4355 S. National #2206, Springfield, MO 65810, (417) 883-6753.

Patricia Lorenz is the author of *Stuff that Matters for Single Parents* and *A Hug a Day for Single Parents,* which can be ordered from Servant Publications by calling 1-800-458-8505. She is a contributing writer for *A 2nd Helping of Chicken Soup for the Soul, A 3rd Serving of Chicken Soup for the Soul, A 4th Course of Chicken Soup for the Soul,* and *Chicken Soup for the Woman's Soul.* She has had over 400 articles published in national magazines such as *Reader's Digest, Guidepost, Working Mother, Woman's World, Single-Parent Family,* and *Mature Outlook.* She's a contributing writer for ten of the *Daily Guideposts* books, a columnist, speaker, and once-in-awhile writing instructor. You can write to her at 7457 S. Pennsylvania Avenue, Oak Creek, WI 53154.

Jessica Magers is a graduate of Billings Central High School, 1996. She studied Spanish and French, and traveled with Close Up to Washington, DC. She writes poetry and hopes to someday publish a book of poems. She also anticipates furthering her education. Jessica can be reached at 1245 Rimrock Road, Billings, MT 5910.

Nailah Malik is a multicultural storyteller, literacy advocate, and young adult librarian of the Los Angeles Public Library. Having triumphed over formidable personal challenges, she brings warmth and passion to her presentations that inspire and empower others. Her emphasis on stories that have practical applications for learning and living has made her a highly sought-after trainer and weaver of tales, and a powerful motivational speaker for students and educators of grade schools, colleges, and universities in

California. She has earned a B.A. in Economics from the University of California, Santa Barbara. Nailah can be reached at P.O. Box 6026-282 Sherman Oaks, CA 91413, or by calling (213) 857-8089.

James Malinchak is one of the nation's most dynamic young speakers and is being called "America's Hottest Young Speaker." He speaks more than 150 times a year to groups of adults, college students, and teenagers presenting his motivational and inspirational talks. He is the author of five motivational books and is a contributing author to the *Chicken Soup for the Soul* book series. To request a product catalog or to schedule him for a speaking engagement please contact: James Malinchak International, P.O. Box 32, Monessen, PA 15062, or call 1-888-793-1196, or E-mail: JamesMal@aol.com, or visit his website at http://www.Malinchak.com.

Tony Overman is a nationally known motivational youth speaker. He founded the National Youth "I Care" Hotline and produced *Teen Talk*, a nine-part video series. Tony conducts training workshops for teachers and motivational assemblies for schools. He can be reached at 18965 F.M. 2252, Garden Ridge, TX 78266, phone (800) 487-8464.

Lawrence Pollard writes inspirational columns. He is also a chaplin at Southside Virginia Training Center, Petersburg, Virginia. He can be reached at 3412 Foster Avenue, Ettrick, Virginia 23803.

Jason Summey speaks regularly about his "Be Cool, Stay in School" program and is currently completing a book on the subject. He can be reached at P.O. Box 16844, Asheville, NC 28816, or by calling (704) 252-3573, Fax (828) 254-7220.

Donna Wick, founder of the Center for Positive Change in Houston, currently conducts a national seminar series, "Awaken the God Within." She has a weekly television series and an extensive background in personal development, motivation, and inspiration. Donna believes that no one was created without purpose in the world and there exists, for all of us, a meaning and mission for our lives. For information on her center, write to 43 Alden Glen, The Woodlands, TX 77382 or call (409) 321-5717.

Amy Yerkes is planning a career in public relations and enjoys writing poetry in her spare time. She can be reached at 50 Rainbow Trail, Denville, NJ 07834, or by calling (201) 625-2690.